The Dogs Are Boiled Alive
While the World Pretends to Care

*A Cry for the Dogs of Yulin
and for the Silence
That Keeps Them Burning*

Sahar Soltani

Copyright © 2025 Sahar Soltani
All rights reserved.

No part of this publication may be reproduced, stored in a retrieval system, or transmitted in any form, electronic, mechanical, photocopying, recording, or otherwise, without prior written permission from the author, except for brief quotations used in reviews, articles, or scholarly works.

Every word, every line, and every cry were born from the author's own heart, mind, and soul drawn from years of handwritten journals with unbearable truths and a bleeding heart for the voiceless no machine could ever give voice to.

Disclaimer:
This book contains graphic and emotionally disturbing content related to animal cruelty including but not limited to the Yulin Dog Meat Festival and similar practices documented in other parts of the world. Reader discretion is strongly advised.

Every act described is grounded in documented reality, based on eyewitness accounts, investigative reports, and verifiable evidence from multiple regions. While presented in a poetic and emotional style, nothing in this work has been invented or fictionalized. This is not speculation. It is a call for awareness, accountability, and change.

Published by The Quiet Seer Press, Toronto, Canada
Cover and interior design by Sahar Soltani
thequietseerpress@outlook.com
Printed and distributed globally via independent publishing services and retail networks.
First Edition. 2025
ISBN: 978-1-0695547-5-8

To those who looked,

but didn't step up.

To those who said, "How terrible,"
and did nothing.

To those I asked for help,
to give voice to the voiceless,
but who kept their own voices instead.

To those who had the power
to change lives,
even the ones they called trivial,
but chose instead to accumulate more dust.
Needlessly.

To the ones who could have spoken,
but delayed.
Until there was no breath left to save.

To the voiceless ones
who couldn't speak,
who couldn't even bark
through the agony,
you will always be remembered.

To the innocent cries that were so loud

they split the silence of Heaven,
I promise you:
they have reached the Creator.
He is honing His lightning sword.
He will avenge you.

You are redeemed.
I promise you.
Not because of my promise,
but because His Word never returns void.

You are redeemed
and will be redeemed
even if the world does not yet understand.
Only the remnant knows.

Your cries may have been deafened
by the so-called humans who looked away,
who defended their ears
with pride and performance.

But your cries reached mine.
And they pierced
and ripped
my heart
into pieces.

You are forever loved.

And you will be forever loved.
You will always be in my heart.

And I will see you all one day
when that time comes,
when we meet our Redeemer:
Yeshua.
               יהושע

The One who never looked away.

I wrote this for you
not because I had the leisure,
but because I didn't have
the kind of power
or wealth
that those ones had.
The ones who could have helped you.
The kind I still pray to one day hold.

And most importantly,
because I cried out for help.
And no one responded.
No one looked.
No one listened.

And so I am here.
Using whatever is left of my voice
to speak for you

and to cry out for you.

Let it be said that I tried.
Let it be said that I remember you,
because the One who formed you
was first pierced for you.

—Sahar Soltani

Table of Contents

Title Page
Copyright Page
Dedication
Table of Contents
Preface: This Is Not Fiction
Before You Ask Me How I Know
Genesis 9:5 — A Divine Warning
Prologue: The Difference Between Feeling and Fire

Chapter 1: The Cry No One Hears.................1
Chapter 2: The World That Pretends to Care..7
Chapter 3: The Dogs Are Boiled Alive...........11

Chapter 4: They Tried to Crawl Out............15
Chapter 5: I Saw Children—Not Just Dogs.....21

Chapter 6: Where Was Everyone?....................25
Chapter 7: The Ones Who Looked Away.......33

Chapter 8: There Is No "Humane" Yulin.......37

Chapter 9: A Scroll for the Forgotten............41
Chapter 10: Let It Be Said That I Tried..........45

What Now: Their Blood Is Still Boiling..........49
Why It Still Happens……………………..............51
The Ones Still Fighting…………………..............55
How You Can Help……………..........……………65
Silent Reflections…………………………...........67
Pierced Reflection.……………………..…...........69
Final Scripture: Deuteronomy 32:41-43……71
The Same Breath: Nefesh and Ruach in All Creation……………………………………..73
Other Works by Sahar Soltani……………….77
About the Author……………………………….79
Acknowledgments………………………….....81

Preface: This Is Not Fiction

What you are about to read
is not poetic metaphor.
It is not dramatization.
It is not exaggeration.

It is real.

Every scream.
Every burn.
Every hammer
that forced a living creature
back into boiling water
happened.

It is happening still.

This book was not written to inspire.
It was written to **witness.**
To record what most people refuse to see.
To cry out what the world scrolls past.

If you find yourself thinking,
"This can't be true—surely not,"
pause.
"This is too hard to read…"

ask yourself:
What more for the ones who had to live it?

You'll find I've already softened
what they endured.
Not exaggerated it.

This is not a story.
This is a scroll

for the **forgotten.**

Before You Ask Me How I Know

I did not stand on the soil of Yulin.
But I didn't need to.
Because I tried.
I asked how.
I searched who.
I begged to go.
I was ready.

I cried out for help.
No one responded.
So I stayed here,
but I did not stay silent.

What you read in this book is not fantasy.
It is fact.
Public footage.
Verified torture.
The screams were recorded.
And still—no one stopped it.

I did not imagine these scenes.
I saw them.
I heard them.
And I haven't been the same since.

I didn't bury their pain.
I carry it.
It lives inside me.

It took something from me.
Joy, that cannot return.

And still, I wrote.
Not to move on.
But to hold them.
To say: I saw you.
I did not forget.

Because silence
was never neutral.
And memory…
is the beginning of justice.

אַךְ אֶת־דִּמְכֶם לְנַפְשֹׁתֵיכֶם אֶדְרֹשׁ

מִיַּד כָּל־חַיָּה אֶדְרְשֶׁנּוּ

וּמִיַּד הָאָדָם מִיַּד אִישׁ אָחִיו

אֶדְרֹשׁ אֶת־נֶפֶשׁ הָאָדָם:

And surely your lifeblood I will require;

from every beast I will require it,

and from man,

from every man's brother

I will require the life of man.

—Genesis 9:5

Prologue: The Difference Between Feeling and Fire

They say they care.
They cry in comment sections.
They repost filtered pain.
They say, "How awful."
And then they go back to eating,
scrolling,
laughing.

Because the world has confused
feeling with action.

They think caring is enough,
but caring without cost
is counterfeit.

They perform outrage,
but they don't intervene.

They wear morality like a coat,
until it gets too hot.
Then they take it off.

That is not compassion.
That is performance.

What True Compassion Looks Like:

True compassion doesn't just feel.
It moves.

It doesn't say, "That's horrible,"
and then go make coffee
like nothing happened.
Or
"That breaks my heart"
then ask,
Can I book you now for your next
appointment?

And no word of 'let me see what I could do' or
'I would love to help or support in any way' I
can but silence.

It doesn't cry for a minute
Then scroll to a sale.

True compassion disrupts your peace.
It changes your day.
Your wallet.
Your schedule.
Your sleep.
Your posture toward the world.

If it costs you nothing,
it's not compassion.
Its theater.

If you felt sadness,
but didn't stop your life
to help
the ones screaming—

you didn't care.
You just watched.

True compassion is inconvenient.
It interrupts your plans.
It wrecks your comfort,
and robs your sleep,
and ignites your conscience.

It moves your feet,
opens your wallet,
or burns through
your silence.

True compassion doesn't care
how it looks.
It cares
who is bleeding.

It leaves you
crying alone on your kitchen floor,
because you couldn't save them.

If your compassion never cost you,
it was never compassion.
It was a costume you wore
until it wrinkled.

So no,
this book is not for the ones
who want to learn more.

This is not just for awareness.
This is for accountability.

Because I tried.
I tried hard.
And no one called back.
No one looked.
No one came.

So now I'm writing it down.
For the record.
For Heaven.

For them.

Chapter 1: The Cry No One Hears

They will ask me,
"Why do you cry for the dogs
while children are dying in Gaza,
in Ukraine, in Israel?"

And I will answer,
not with defense,
but with truth.

Because what is happening to the dogs in Yulin
is deliberate.
Not the collateral of war.
Not a tragedy of conflict.
But a ritualized torment,
planned,
approved,
and celebrated.

Because they are alive
when they are thrown
into boiling pots.

Because they are aware when
their limbs are snapped
and their throats are burned.

Because they scream the way
any child would,
and no one listens.

I am not saying human suffering doesn't
matter.
I'm saying this matters too.
And no one seems to be saying it.

This is not about choosing between
dog and child.

This is about choosing between
silence and truth.
Between apathy
and action.
Between scrolling on
and letting your soul stop cold.

I do cry for children.
I long to rescue the trafficked,
the tortured,
the North Korean child
born behind walls
no one dares tear down.

I cry for the ones in red rooms,

whose screams are sold as entertainment.
Who are never found,
because no one dares to look.

I cry for the child lying on a table.
prepared like a meal for a ritual.
Stabbed in secret.
Served in silence.
Buried in stories the world dismisses
as "conspiracy,"
but are real to the child
who never walked out.

There are too many.
Too many cries
behind closed doors.
Too many victims
wrapped in shadows.

But right now,
this is the cry
that has gripped
my lungs.

But this,
this agony of the dogs
is one I'm allowed
to speak about.

One I can cry out against publicly.
And even this—
even this—
the world still
refuses to stop.

Not because it is more important.
But because it is more forgotten.

Because it is more invisible.
Because people say,
"How awful"
and then do nothing.

The world has confused
feeling
with compassion.

Caring is not conviction.
Outrage without action
is counterfeit.
Morality without cost
is performance.

So let it be said:
I did not look away.
I did not say "how sad" and scroll on.

I am using
what's left of my breath
to speak for those
who have none.

Let the world misunderstand me.
Let them question my heart.

But let the record show:

I tried.

Chapter 2: The World That Pretends to Care

They share the posts.
They wear the slogans.
They say, "This needs to stop."
But then they go back to dinner.
To comfort.
To sleep.

The outrage is digital.
The agony is real.

They will say, "We didn't know."
But they did.
They just didn't care enough
to remember.

Many saw the footage.
Heard the screams.
Felt that flicker of conscience
and drowned it with noise.

This world performs empathy,
but doesn't carry it.

It displays pain like fashion
until it's out of season.
Their mercy follows trends,
a diet they try for a week,
a jacket they wear for a season,
never a skin they live in.

You cried when a fictional animal died
in a movie,
but looked away from the dog
who was skinned alive
in real life.

You reposted awareness,
but didn't send a single dollar.
Didn't write a single email.
Didn't even stop to pray.

You say, "This breaks my heart."
But hearts that are truly broken
don't move on.
They bleed.
They break again
and again.

The truth is:
most people don't care
until it's convenient.

Until it's trending.
Until they can do it safely
from their screen.

But compassion
without cost
isn't compassion.
It's ego.

Justice that doesn't disturb your peace
isn't justice.
It's branding.

You cared just enough
to feel good about yourself.
Not enough to stop
the suffering.

And this is what we mean
when we say

the world

pretends

to care.

Chapter 3: The Dogs Are Boiled Alive

They don't die quickly.
They don't die quietly.
And they don't die
because anyone had to eat.

They are boiled
alive.

Thrown in—
conscious.
Eyes wide.
Limbs tied.

Some screaming,
some shaking,
some still hoping to be spared
until the very last second.

The pot hisses.
The lid slams.
And the body inside thrashes,
burning from the inside out,
but not dead yet.

This is not food.

This is a ritual of dominance.
Of consumption as cruelty.
Of breaking something
while it still breathes,
just to feel power.

They say it's "tradition."
They say the meat is "more potent"
when the dog dies afraid.
As if pain is a spice.
As if agony is an ingredient.

This isn't culture.
This is evil.
This is demonic.
And it is celebrated.

They walk through cages and point.
"Pick that one."
The white one.
The scared one.
The one who's still wagging her tail,
because she thinks someone
has finally come
to take her home.

But they don't take her home.
They take her to the pot.

Still breathing.
Still believing.

They don't just suffer.
They try to escape.

They claw at the sides.
They lunge their burned bodies toward the rim,
eyes wide,
muzzles blistered,
legs trembling from heat and terror,
because even in that agony
they still want to live.

And when they almost make it out,
they are not pulled up.
They are hammered back in.

Not to end it.
Not to kill them.
But to force them to stay awake.
To make them feel more.

More fire.
More betrayal.
More human hands
choosing not mercy
but domination.

And we dare call this meat!
Dare call it culture!
And still pretend
it's distant or complicated.

No.
This is calculated torment.
It is evil.
And the worst part?
It isn't hidden.

It's posted.
Recorded.
Laughed at.
Watched.

While the world
scrolls on.

Chapter 4: They Tried to Crawl Out

They didn't just suffer.
They tried to escape.

They wanted to live.

Burned,
blistered,
half-boiled,
they still clawed at the edge.

They pulled what was left of their bodies up,
desperate,
trembling,
eyes wide with a kind of terror
no being should ever know,
and somehow,
they still believed
someone might save them.

They almost made it out.
Their paws reached the rim.
Their mouths gaped for air,
not from instinct,
but from hope.

They were awake.
Still conscious.
Still fighting for life.

But then—

The hammer.

Not to end their pain,
but to push them back in.
To keep them alive.

To make them feel more.

More fire.
More fear.
More betrayal.

Their skulls were not crushed.
They were pressed.
Bludgeoned.
Not to silence their screams
but to prolong them.

This is not slaughter.
This is ritual torment.
It is evil.
And it is done on purpose.

They were not put to death.
They were kept from dying.

And that is the worst kind of cruelty:
not pain that ends
but pain that is preserved,
extended,
reheated,
dragged out,
because someone decided
that fear would make the meat taste better.

Some of them stopped screaming.
Not because they lost consciousness
but because they gave up.

Because they realized
no one was coming.

They stopped clawing.
They stopped gasping.
They just stared
silent,
wide-eyed,
as the heat devoured
what was left of them.

They died awake.

They died knowing the hand
that touched them
was not love,
not rescue,
not even death,
but power.

This is not about food.
It never was.

It's about control.
It's about who gets to live,
and who gets to beg
for death.

And the world
knows.

They have seen the videos.
They have heard the screams.
They have watched the footage
of a dog's burned face
rising from the pot—
only to be shoved back under by human hands
with no urgency to kill,
only a hunger to dominate.

The worst part is not that it happened.
It's that it keeps happening.

And still,
no one came.

Not for them.
Not in time.
Not even once.

Chapter 5: I Saw Children — Not Just Dogs

Where others saw dogs,
I saw children.

Not because they looked like children,
but because they trusted like them.
Cried like them.
Trembled like them.
Hoped like them,
until hope turned into horror.

They didn't bark to fight.
They whimpered to ask.
To ask for a hand,
for a lap,
for a home.

They believed they were being rescued
as the cage door opened.
They wagged their tails
not because they were dumb,
but because they were good.

Like a child,
they didn't know the world

would betray them.
They didn't know that trust
could be fatal.

And I couldn't look away.
Because once I saw it,
I couldn't unsee it.

I couldn't separate their scream
from the sound of a baby's cry.
I couldn't separate their eyes
from the eyes of the trafficked,
the tortured,
the ones hidden in basements
no one will ever search.

I didn't see "animals."
I saw innocence.
I saw the *least of these*.

And when I saw them broken,
bleeding,
trying to crawl out of hell—
I didn't just cry.

I remembered Him.
Because He said it clearly:
"Whatever you did

for the least of these…
you did for Me."
—Matthew 25:40

And though these words were first spoken over
the suffering of humankind,
His heart has always seen
the lamb, the sparrow, the ox, the hound,
for He is not bound by our limits,
and He holds the lifeblood to account,
even for the beasts we call nothing.
For He is the one and only
Creator of them all.

But the world didn't.
They saw fur,
not feeling.
Meat,
not memory.
Profit,
not personhood.

And so they walked away
untouched.
Unaffected.
Unmoved.

But I stayed.

I let their agony
rewire my vision.

Because they weren't "just dogs."
They were like
children.

And like every child
who has ever suffered in silence,
they were in YHWH's heart.

And yes,
Including
beasts...

Chapter 6: Where Was Everyone?

I tried.
I posted.
I called.
I wept.
I begged.

And no one came.

Not the ones who repost everything.
Not the ones who say
they care about justice.
Not the ones who share war headlines
and sign petitions for all the "right" causes.
Not even the ones I called directly
who said they were heartbroken,
then went silent.

Where were they
when the dogs screamed?

They weren't hiding.
They weren't unaware.
They saw the clips.
They heard the screams.
They read the captions.

They watched the footage
long enough to whisper,
"I can't watch this."
And then they moved on.

And that is the lie of this generation.
They call it compassion,
but it's only compassion
until it gets too heavy.

Until it disrupts their comfort.
Until it costs them followers.
Until it stains their aesthetic.

They cry for Gaza.
They cry for Ukraine.
They cry for climate.
They cry for Palestine.
They cry for oceans and trees
and women's rights
and stolen lands—
as they should.

But when it comes to dogs
being boiled alive—
silence.

Why?

Because it's inconvenient.
Because it's graphic.
Because it's uncomfortable.

Because they would rather say,
"I just can't look at that,"
than admit:
"I don't care enough to help."

The Yulin Dog Meat Festival
has been happening
since 2009.
The world has known about it
for over a decade.

Activists have screamed.
Videos have been shared.
Celebrities have posted.
Organizations have protested.

And still, it continues.

The Chinese government says
it doesn't support it.
But it lets it happen.
In broad daylight.
Every June.

Thousands of dogs.
Caged.
Burned.
Beaten.
Boiled.
Skinned.
Alive.

And the world?
Said "That's awful."
And did nothing.

Where was everyone?

Where were you
when the dogs were screaming,
their paws pressed to the edge of the pot,
their bodies trying to escape the boil?

Where were you
when I was crying in my room,
writing,
posting,
pleading,
and no one responded?

You were online.
You were active.

You were watching.

You just didn't stay.

This chapter isn't written in bitterness.
It's written in grief.

Because I believed you.
I believed you when you said
you cared.
When you said
justice mattered.
When you said,
"We must speak for the voiceless."

But when the voiceless had fur,
you disappeared.

There is no such thing
as passive innocence
in the face of torment.

You either helped
stop it
or you let it
continue.

And that is why

I am writing this.

Because silence

is **never**

neutral.

Rescue those
being taken away to death,
hold back those
stumbling toward slaughter.
If you say,
"Look, we did not know this,"
does not He who weighs the heart
consider it?
And does not He who keeps your soul
know it?
And will He not repay each one
according to his deeds?

—Proverbs 24:11-12

Chapter 7: The Ones Who Looked Away

They heard.
They saw.
They just didn't stay.

They clicked away
before the scream finished.

They turned down the volume.
They changed the channel.
And then they changed nothing.

They will say,
"I didn't know."
But they did.
And YHWH knows
they did.

Because the scream was loud.
The blood was public.
The torture wasn't hidden.
Only ignored.

What kind of world keeps scrolling
while something burns alive?

What kind of people say,
"That's sad,"
and then do nothing with the sadness?

There were thousands who saw
but only a remnant who wept.
And fewer still who acted.

They reposted horror
to decorate their conscience,
then returned to normal
as if they didn't just witness murder.

No, this was not ignorance.
It was willful apathy.
It was moral abandonment.

And what does YHWH say?
"Will He not repay each one
according to his deeds?"

Because justice remembers.
Because lifeblood speaks.

Because silence has weight.

Let no one say again,
"I didn't know."
Let no one pretend
they did not see.

The only thing missing…
was sacrifice.
And without sacrifice,
compassion was only
a pose.

Because where there is no cost,
there was no compassion.

And where there was no compassion,
there will be no excuse.
No mercy.
Only judgment.

Chapter 8: There Is No "Humane" Yulin

They try to defend it.
They say it's culture.
They say, "But not all of them boil the dogs alive."
They say, "Some die quickly."
As if that justifies anything.

But Yulin is not a meal.
It's not a market.
It is a ritual of torment.
Dogs are not simply killed,
they are tortured on purpose.

Because pain is part of the myth.
Because fear makes the meat "stronger."
Because suffering, in this festival,
is not a side effect—
it's the goal.

They are burned.
Beaten.
Skinned.
Boiled.
Mocked.

Alive.

And when one tries to climb out of the pot—
boiled skin sliding from his legs,
gasping, still alive—
they hammer him back in.

Not to end his life.
But to prolong his pain.

That is Yulin.

And Yulin is not confined
to a single week in June.
The slaughter does not pause
when the festival ends.

Across China, Vietnam,
dogs are burned,
beaten,
boiled,
and butchered in the same ways,
every day of the year.

The trade reaches beyond these borders
into Cambodia, South Korea, Indonesia,
but nowhere is the cruelty so celebrated,

so ritualized,
as in the killing fields of Yulin.

Yulin is not a date on the calendar.
It is a mindset,
an illegal trade,
a ritualized torture,
cruelly celebrated and filmed.

And there is no humane version of it.
No cultural excuse.
No "cleaner method."
No softened language can justify this.

Many were stolen from homes.
Still wearing collars.
Some were waiting for someone to come.
And no one did.

Now their bodies hang like displays.
Their fur burned off.
Their mouths silent.
Their memory erased
by a world that dares to call it
"tradition."

But it is not tradition.
It is pure evil.

And the worst part is this:
the world knows.
And this horror still continues
in this day and age.

Let no one say,
"Maybe it's not as bad as they say."
It is worse.

There is no "kind death" at Yulin.
Only fire,
fear,
and screams.

Let it be said plainly:
There is no such thing
as humane killing
in a place built to glorify suffering.

Mercy is found nowhere
in Yulin
or in the countless places
that mirrors its cruelty.

Chapter 9: A Scroll for the Forgotten

You were real.
You were not numbers.
You were not meat.
You were not noise.

You were souls.

You waited at doorsteps.
You slept beneath carts.
You wagged your tails for people
who never deserved your trust.

You licked the hands
that would later bind you.
You followed voices
that led you into cages.
And you still believed,
even when the metal slammed behind you
that someone might come for you.

But no one came.

No one came
before the pot boiled.
Before the hammer fell.

Before your screams
were posted online
and watched like entertainment.

You were forgotten
by a world that claims to be "aware."
You were erased
by people who say they care.

But I have written you here.
Every cry that was never answered,
every paw that scratched the air,
every eye that searched for mercy
is now inside this scroll.

You are recorded.
You are remembered.
You are not gone.

Heaven saw you.
He saw you.

YHWH heard the scream
no one else would hear.
And while the world scrolled,
He stood.

He did not flinch.

He did not turn away.
He watched every breath
you were denied.

Because the blood they spilled
speaks even now.
And He holds them accountable
And will hold them still
on the final day.

And His judgment is etched
in His book,
engraved on His heart.

Because you were not nothing.
You were
the *least of these*.

—

And I,

will not let the world forget

what they tried to erase.

I will make them

remember.

Chapter 10: Let It Be Said That I Tried

I didn't have money.
I didn't have reach.
I didn't have a platform,
a foundation,
a sponsor,
or the strength to fly there myself.

But I had my voice.
And I used it.

I had my tears.
And I let them fall.

I had my pen.
And I wrote.

While others said, "That's awful,"
and moved on—
I stayed.

I screamed in silence.
I begged strangers to care.
I prayed for a miracle no one else believed in.

And when nothing changed,

I wrote this.

Not to feel better.
Not to heal.
But to testify.

Let it be said that I tried.

Let it be written
that I did not look away.

That when the world chose silence,
I chose to speak.

When they said, "It's just too much,"
I said, "Imagine being the one living it."

When they muted the video,
I raised my voice.

When they turned off the screen,
I turned to the page.

I could not save them.
But I could say their names.
I could hold their memory.
I could scream into paper
so their cries would not die in the air.

This scroll is not a solution.
It's a witness.

It's a record for the day
when justice rolls down like fire
and YHWH asks the question:

"Where were you
when the least of these screamed?"

And may I answer without shame:

"I was here.
I was writing.
I was weeping.
I was warning.
I was standing where they fell."

Let it be said
that Sahar
remembered them.

—

Because He

was **first pierced**

for them.

What Now: Their Blood Is Still Boiling

If you close this book and do nothing,

then they really did die in vain.

—Sahar Soltani

Why It Still Happens

The Yulin Dog Meat Festival is not a centuries-old tradition.
It began in 2009, created purely for profit, violence, and false pride.

Every year in Asia, tens of millions of dogs, and millions more cats
are slaughtered for meat.

In China alone, around 10 million dogs
are consumed yearly.
In Vietnam, Cambodia, and Indonesia,
another estimated 10 million dogs and cats
are killed annually.

In Indonesia, this trade is not nationwide.
It is concentrated in certain non-Muslim communities in regions like North Sulawesi, North Sumatra, and East Nusa Tenggara.

Even so, around 1 million dogs are killed each year, including 60,000–70,000 in Bali alone.

While the majority of Indonesians reject the practice, 93% support a ban,

those who keep it alive still deal in cruelty and death.
In Vietnam alone, one of the world's highest consumers, **around 5 million dogs and 1 million cats** are stolen, trafficked, and slaughtered each year.

Brutal methods are common: **bludgeoning, burning alive, throat-slitting in makeshift markets.**
The animals are not "livestock"—**many begin as pets.**
And yet, despite growing revulsion, the practice persists, embedded in custom and profit.

And this does not include the thousands (or more) lost each day in markets, farms, and illegal trade.

Many are stolen and **still wearing collars.**
Others are strays, trafficked across borders, or bred in brutal conditions.

They are crammed into cages too small to stand.
Beaten with rods to "tenderize" the meat.
Burned alive for "flavor".
Boiled screaming.
Skinned while conscious.

This is not a myth.
Not exaggerated.
It is real
And it continues.

Why?

Because silence is profitable.
Because governments turn away.
Because people hide behind the word "culture"
to avoid confrontation.
Because the media chooses easier stories.
Because the world forgets fast
and corporations move faster.

And because when we look away…
they die unheard.

But this is not someone else's problem.

It's ours.

The Ones Still Fighting

Yang Xiaoyun
The Woman Who Would Not Look Away

A retired schoolteacher from Tianjin, China, Yang Xiaoyun has poured her life, her personal savings, and her soul into rescuing dogs from the horror of the meat trade.

She has reportedly saved over 1,000 dogs, not through an organization, but through her own two hands, her home, and her heart.

She has traveled across provinces, sometimes for days, to reach slaughterhouses and meat markets before the killing began.

In one image that circulated globally in 2015, she is seen kneeling on the ground, weeping and begging a man to sell her his dog instead of slaughtering it.
She carried only a small amount of cash and all the hope she had left.

But she never stopped.

Yang built her own sanctuary in Tianjin, where she houses hundreds of rescued dogs.
She cooks for them daily.
She sits with the traumatized ones.
She mourns those she cannot save.
And through it all, she continues with no fame, no fortune, and no safety net but only resolve.

She has said she hopes to continue saving dogs until the end of her life. Her unwavering commitment has made her a powerful and respected figure in the fight for animal welfare in China. And those who know her work believe this too: She will give her last breath to protect theirs.

Wang Yan

Formerly a millionaire from Helong City, Wang Yan's life changed forever when his own dog went missing in 2012.
His search led him to a slaughterhouse, where he witnessed unspeakable cruelty.

Determined to intervene, he bought a facility and transformed it into the **Changchun Animal Rescue Base.**

Since then, he has rescued over 2,000 dogs, investing his entire fortune into their care and refusing personal donations but only accepting supplies for the animals.

Chef Wang

A former professional chef in China, Chef Wang made an extraordinary decision after witnessing the cruelty of the dog meat trade. Instead of continuing his culinary career, he turned his life upside down, not for profit, but for compassion.

He began adopting stray, abandoned, and vulnerable dogs, many of whom were at risk of being captured, sold and then slaughtered. Over time, his home became a sanctuary. He often uses his own savings to cover medical care, shelter upgrades, and food, never asking for recognition but only asking that the killing stop.

But he didn't stop there.

He now cooks fresh, homemade meals for over a hundred rescued dogs every single day,

treating them not as property, but as souls
worthy of love, warmth, and dignity.

His quiet act of rebellion has been covered in
international media, but he seeks no fame, only
peace for the ones who cannot speak.

Chef Wang stands as a living contradiction to
the culture of cruelty around him:
Once a man who cooked for people,
Now a man who protects those
who were almost served as food.

His life a recipe of defiance, compassion, and
redemption, one bowl of rice, one rescued life at
a time.

Wang Yanfang
The Guardian of 1,300 Strays

In 2009, the local government in Weinan,
Shaanxi Province ordered the mass killing of
stray dogs, not out of mercy, but to "clean the
streets."

No rescue.
No rehabilitation.
No evaluation.

Just mass killing. Fast, cheap, and quiet.

Stray dogs were rounded up by authorities and slaughtered by the hundreds.
These operations were state-sanctioned and indiscriminate, targeting every dog in sight regardless of health or behaviour.
Methods included poisoning, blunt force trauma,
and electrocution.
No vetting. No triage. No exceptions.

Even friendly, healthy, and adoptable dogs, **some still wearing collars**, were exterminated alongside the rest.
Their lives ended not because they were dangerous,
But because they were unwanted.

Wang Yanfang refused.

She stood in the gap and built a shelter with her bare hands.

Alongside a group of elderly women, she now cares for over 1,300 dogs.

They rise at 4 a.m. daily to cook and carry nearly 400 kilograms of food.
They do not rest.
They do not forget.
They do not turn away.

They chose compassion over compliance and gave life where the system had chosen death.

Her honour is not in what she built.
It's in what she refused to let be destroyed.

Duo Duo Project

A U.S.-based nonprofit focused on ending the dog meat trade through education, advocacy, local reform, and pressure campaigns to stop the trade. They support grassroots activists, fund rescues and work directly with communities across Asia.

Humane Society International

Working globally to end the dog meat trade through political pressure, undercover investigations, rescue missions, and public awareness campaigns.

They partner with local organizations to shut down slaughterhouses and transition former dog meat farmers into humane livelihoods.

No Dogs Left Behind
An International Rescue Effort

Founded by Jeffrey Beri, No Dogs Left Behind is a global nonprofit organization that collaborates with Chinese activists to rescue dogs directly from trucks, wet markets and slaughterhouses.

They operate sanctuaries in Dayi and Gongyi, providing urgent medical care, rehabilitation, and adoption services for dogs once marked for death.

Their mission is relentless: to expose and dismantle the systems that profit off torture and silence.

Their efforts have saved thousands of animals and continue to raise global awareness about the atrocities of the dog meat industry.

NoToDogMeat

Among the organizations I reached out to, NoToDogMeat was the only one that responded with genuine care. I support their cause not only because of their commitment to the dogs, but because they fight with a relentless dedication that inspires action. I believe in their mission. I admire Julia and her team for their tireless work and the countless hours they devote as volunteers, without expecting recognition or reward.

At the time of writing, I am gathering a protest, not alone this time, but with others who refuse to remain silent. This is not symbolic. This is strategic. If we gather enough people, the media will have no choice but to cover us, and that coverage will travel all the way to Xi's seat, and to the Vietnamese government.

Join us.
Your presence is not just welcomed, it is needed. Every single person who shows up increases our chances of being seen, being heard, and forcing the issue into the spotlight. The more we stand together, the more impossible it becomes for them to ignore us.

If you are reading this before the protest, come. Stand with us. Let the world see that the dogs have defenders.

If you are reading this after the protest has passed, the mission is not over. There will be another stand, another march, another chance to add your voice to the chorus demanding change. Stay ready. Stay willing.

Join us—now, or in the next wave. **But join us.**

If you are reading this before the protest, contact me right away to join us. My email is listed on the copyright page of this book. Write "Protest" in the subject line so it stands out.
My team and I will get back to you with the details.

How You Can Help

1. **Don't stay silent.**
   Silence is fuel for the fire.
   Share this book.
   Spread the truth.
   Be louder than the ones who pretend this isn't happening.

2. **Support those on the front lines.**
   Fund real rescues.
   Follow.
   Amplify their work:
   - **NoToDogMeat: notodogmeat.com**
   - Duo Duo Project: duoduoproject.org
   - Humane Society International: his.org
   - No Dogs Left Behind: nodogsleftbehind.com

3. **Disrupt the apathy.**
   Email officials.
   Tag politicians.
   Protest peacefully.
   Post unapologetically.
   Make it impossible for them to ignore.
   And most of all, JOIN OUR PROTEST.

4. **Put your money where their survival is.**
   Every cent can pull a dog off a truck,
   out of a cage,
   or away from a blade.

   Don't underestimate the lives
   what your giving can save.

5. **Go where the pain is.**
   If you have the means—**go.**
   Stand at the gates.
   Bear witness with your own eyes.
   Join the rescues.
   Document the horror.
   Be the human shield they never had.

   Even one dog spared from the blade
   is a future changed forever.

   Because silence dies
   When someone **dares to show up.**

Silent Reflections

What broke you the most in this book and
why did it hurt that deep?

What truth can you no longer unsee?

What will you do now that ignorance is
no longer an option?

If this were your dog, stolen, tortured, silenced,
what would you want the world to do?

Will you be the one who walks away…
or the one who returns with fire?

If you stay silent now…
what part of you dies with them?

Can you still look at them the same,
or did something sacred shift in you too?

Pierced Reflection

Boiled, but Not Silenced
You burned them.
But the flame spread.

Yang's Hands
Her hands shake.
Her knees ache.
But she kneels anyway.
And when no one else shows up,
she does.

One More Bark
They barked until their throats broke.
So now, we speak.

You are no longer innocent.
So now—be unignorable.

—S.S.

If I sharpen My flashing sword
and My hand takes hold on judgment,
I will take vengeance on My adversaries
and repay those who hate Me.
I will make My arrows drunk with blood,
and My sword shall devour flesh…
Rejoice, O nations, with His people,
for He will avenge the blood of His
servants,
and take vengeance on His adversaries.
He will provide atonement
for His land
and His people.

—Deuteronomy 32:41-43

The Same Breath: Nefesh and Ruach in All Creation

What Was Breathed into Adam…
was Also Breathed into the Beast.

רֵאשִׁית א:כ–כא
יִשְׁרְצוּ הַמַּיִם שֶׁרֶץ נֶפֶשׁ חַיָּה...
וַיִּבְרָא אֱלֹהִים... אֶת כָּל נֶפֶשׁ הַחַיָּה

Let the waters swarm with living beings
(nefesh chayyah) …
And God created every living soul.
Genesis 1:20-21

בְּרֵאשִׁית ב:ז
וַיִּפַּח בְּאַפָּיו נִשְׁמַת חַיִּים
וַיְהִי הָאָדָם לְנֶפֶשׁ חַיָּה

He breathed into his nostrils the breath of life,
and the man became a living soul.
("Living soul" is the same phrase used for
animals, nefesh chayyah.)
Genesis 2:7

קֹהֶלֶת ג:יט—כא
רוּחַ אֶחָת לַכֹּל...
רוּחַ בְּנֵי הָאָדָם...
וְרוּחַ הַבְּהֵמָה

One spirit (ruach) is in all,
the spirit of man…
and the spirit of the beast.
Ecclesiastes 3:19

תְּהִלִּים קד:כט—ל
תֹּסֵף רוּחָם יִגְוָעוּן
תְּשַׁלַּח רוּחֲךָ יִבָּרֵאוּן

You take away their breath,
they perish.
You send forth Your Spirit,
they are created.

ἡ γὰρ ἀποκαραδοκία τῆς κτίσεως
τὴν ἀποκάλυψιν τῶν υἱῶν τοῦ θεοῦ
ἀπεκδέχεται.
τῇ γὰρ ματαιότητι ἡ κτίσις ὑπετάγη…
ἐπ' ἐλπίδι ὅτι καὶ αὐτὴ ἡ κτίσις

ἐλευθερωθήσεται ἀπὸ τῆς δουλείας τῆς
φθορᾶς
εἰς τὴν ἐλευθερίαν τῆς δόξης τῶν τέκνων τοῦ
θεοῦ.
οἴδαμεν γὰρ ὅτι πᾶσα ἡ κτίσις
συστενάζει καὶ συνωδίνει ἄχρι τοῦ νῦν.
Ρωμαίους 8:19–22

For the creation waits in eager expectation
for the revealing of the sons of God.
The creation itself will be set free
from its bondage to decay
and brought into the glorious freedom
of the children of God.
The whole creation has been groaning
as in the pains of childbirth, until now.
Romans 8:19–22

Every creature has nefesh (soul).

Every spirit came from YHWH,

and it will return to Him.

Other Works by Sahar Soltani

You Don't Fit In: *Because the Surface World Cannot Handle Discerning Minds*
A guide for the misfits, the spiritually sensitive, and those never meant to blend in.

You Don't Fit In: (Children's Edition)
Because the Surface World Cannot Handle Discerning Minds. A self-empowering guide for kids and teens who feel different and who is misunderstood. This book helps them see their uniqueness as strength, teaching confidence, courage, and how to stand against bullying and peer pressure without losing who they are.

Unmasking the Trinity Yeshua Is Yahweh:
The Oneness That Was Hidden All Along
A bold return to the original truth: Yeshua is not a separate person of God but He is YHWH.

God, Why Does It Feel Like You Do Not Exist? I Am Dawn: *A Cry for Yulin in a World That's Breaking*

A spiritual scroll for those walking through darkness, wrestling with silence, and awakening to who Yeshua truly is.

The Undefiled One: The Ancient of Days Who Trampled Decay

A theological unveiling of the physical and spiritual purity of Yeshua, utterly undefiled, wholly divine.

The Restoration of 4 Ezra (2 Esdras) Recovered for the Remnant: *A Faithful Reconstruction of YHWH's Word Based on Surviving Manuscripts*

A prophetic unveiling of the apocalyptic vision given to Ezra, faithfully restored from suppressed and fragmented manuscripts calling the remnant to discernment, endurance, and hope.

Mind Game: The Global Web of Gaslighting: How Systems, Institutions, and People Distort Your Reality

Exposing how systems, institutions, and people distort your reality and how to reclaim your mind.

About the Author

Sahar Soltani is not a voice of comfort.
She is a cry in the wilderness.

Her words are not written for applause,
but for remembrance.
For the ones the world forgets.
For the ones who bled without justice.

She has authored works
that expose deception,
call for awakening,
and restore what has been erased.

Both her life and her writing
are dedicated to truth,
no matter the cost.

She is a mother to two children,
and two Samoyeds,
just as dear to her
as her own.

To her, the suffering of a dog
is no different than
the suffering of a child.

And this unbearable truth
compels her to speak,
even when the world
remains silent.

She believes YHWH sees,
remembers,
and will return
with fire in His eyes.

Because **Yeshua is YHWH**.

*And **His Word***

never

returns void.

Acknowledgments

To the dogs of Yulin
and every other dog in this world
that has been tortured,
skinned,
boiled,
burned,
or massacred by us,
this was for you.

To the ones who stayed silent
when I cried for help,
thank you.
Your silence revealed the truth.

To the ones who pretended to care,
who wore empathy
like a mask
but did nothing,
you were never kind.
Only comfortable.

Your compassion was counterfeit.
Your outrage was hollow.
Your silence was violence.

To the few who listened,
you were a whisper of mercy
in the middle of fire.

You will not be forgotten.
You are not gone.
You are recorded.

And your cries have reached
the One whose sword is
already drawn.

To the Uncreated One
who put this fire in me,
a fire the world cannot comprehend
and yet, still pierces me
until my last breath.

YHWH Yeshua,
may You end their suffering.
May You release their breath
back to You,
so I may finally have peace.
Peace that is only when this divine breath
is also returned
to the One who gave it.